SELF-PUBLISHING 3.0

ORNA A. ROSS

ALLIANCE OF INDEPENDENT AUTHORS

INTRODUCTION

ABOUT THIS BOOK

ABOUT THE ALLIANCE OF INDEPENDENT AUTHORS
WRITING, PUBLISHING, AND BUSINESS CRAFT

Our organisation's work is fourfold:

- ALLi *advises*, providing **best-practice information and education** through a Self-Publishing Advice Center that offers a daily blog, weekly livestreams and podcasts, and a bookstore of self-publishing guidebooks and a quarterly member magazine.
- ALLi *monitors* the self-publishing sector through a **watchdog desk**, alerting authors to bad actors and predatory players and running an approved partner program.
- ALLi *campaigns* for the **advancement of indie authors** in the publishing and literary sectors globally (bookstores, libraries, literary events, prizes, grants, awards, and other author organizations), encouraging the provision of publishing and business skills for authors, speaking out against iniquities, and furthering the indie author cause wherever possible.
- ALLi *empowers* independent authors through a wide variety of **member tools and resources** including author forums, contract advice, sample agreements, contacts and networking, literary agency representation, and a member care desk.

Whether you are just starting out or are already an experienced publisher of your own work, ALLi aims to support you every step of the way.

Each individual self-publisher is part of a great contemporary flowering of creative expression in the literary arts. When an author, a group, or a company joins ALLi, they are not just joining an organization but a movement. A chaotic, kaleidoscopic, liberating, exciting, and self-organizing movement that is transforming authorship and publishing from the grassroots up.

If you're an author or self-publishing service and you haven't yet signed up, we'd love to have you join our alliance. Find out more at:

AllianceIndependentAuthors.org

WHAT IS SELF-PUBLISHING 3.0?

This book is all about today's self-publishing authors. Their writing and publishing ambitions. How they make their books. How they reach their readers. How they build income and influence though creative enterprise. It is based on the work of the Alliance of Independent Authors (ALLi) and the experience of that association's members, team and advisors—including my own.

I am an indie author and poet and in 2012 my co-director (and husband) Philip Lynch and I launched ALLi at the London Book Fair. It quickly grew to be a large global organization, with thousands of members all over the world.

The name ALLi is pronounced "ally" (al-eye), as that's what the association aims to be: the self-publisher's ally. Members are like the three musketeers in Dumas's eponymous novel: each individual ("i") working for the larger ALL. The experience of ALLi's members and advisors is woven into everything our organization does and everything you'll read in this book. Thanks are due to each and all.

When ALLi launched, we were not aware that we were an outgrowth of a publishing era, now called Self-Publishing 2.0, launched by e-book technology. Our experience in the intervening years enabled us to see where the self-publishing movement fitted into publishing history and what that meant for authors who (want to) publish their own work. You.

By the time Self-Publishing 3.0 was dawning, we could see clearly what was going on and what it meant for authors and publishers of all sizes.

So Self-Publishing 3.0 is both a **concept** and a publishing **era** defined by that concept. And it is also an ALLi **campaign** (see #selfpub3.0 on Twitter) that aims to support and accelerate any trends emerging in this era that are advantageous to authors.

The **Self-Publishing 3.0 concept** is that any author (with the requisite writing and publishing skills) now has the means to establish a self-directed, digital business that can be successful, sustainable, and scalable.

The **Self-Publishing 3.0 era,** the era of author enterprise, began around 2018. In this era, writers are moving beyond exclusively signing all rights to a single third-party publisher, or exclusively self-publishing with one platform or service, into true creative and commercial independence.

The Alliance of Independent Author's **Self-Publishing 3.0 campaign** works with authors, readers, literary organizations, and creative industries to support independent authors in acquiring the three necessary skills: writing, publishing, and creative business.

The aims of the campaign are:

1. To alert authors to the full implications of digital publishing and creative business—which go way beyond the much-discussed "choice" between self-publishing versus an exclusive contract with an individual trade publisher.
2. To encourage independent authors to publish widely in as many formats, platforms, and territories as possible, while selling directly to readers and collaborating with other authors.
3. To advise author representative associations and agencies, creative industry bodies, and literacy and cultural organizations across seven key territories (Australia and New

Zealand, Canada, EU, South Africa, the UK, and the USA) on the needs of independent authors.
4. To educate readers on how best to connect with and support independent authors and their books.

Self-Publishing 3.0 requires a major attitudinal and behavorial shift for authors, and for other players in the publishing ecosystem who traditionally view writers as content providers to third-party publishers.

The impact of Self-publishing 3.0 will be defined by the number of authors who take up the opportunity to develop the requisite publishing and business skills and the quality of their work.

This short book outlines why **Self-Publishing 3.0** is important for authors and how to take part in this movement that is enabling writers to earn a living from writing and publishing books.

A NOTE ABOUT PRONOUNS
THE SINGULAR "THEY"

Like all ALLi guides, this book uses **they** and **their** as singular pronouns, rather than **he** and **him** or **she** and **her**, a style choice based on common spoken usage, inclusivity, lexical elegance, and long literary pedigree (good enough for Shakespeare and Jane Austen, to name but two).

ALLi supports the movement to give this pronoun usage contemporary authority. You can read more about that movement and its history at: ornaross.com/singular-they

PART I
AUTHOR INCOME & INDEPENDENCE

CHAPTER 1
THE ENTERPRISING AUTHOR

Every era has seen entrepreneurial authors attracted to the process of publishing and authors' business skills and acumen have been expressed in a variety of ways across centuries. To name but three: Jane Austen's father offering to pay a publishing house to issue the book that would become *Pride and Prejudice* in the 18th century; Charles Dickens making the equivalent of millions in today's money from his stage shows, repurposed content, and multiple streams of income in the 19th century; Leonard and Virginia Woolf's setting up Hogarth Press in the 20th century to publish their own works and those of their friends. For the majority of authors in the age of the printing press, however, the investment of time and money needed to publish effectively was a deterrent.

Then digital publishing technology arrived, in the early 21st century, , changing everything for authors.

Digital publishing does a number of important things that are very good for authors interested in self-publishing. It does away with "out-of-print," making books continually available in three formats: e-books, audiobooks, and POD (print-on-demand). It provides a global readership instead of confining publication to specific territories. It takes away the necessity for intermediaries like agents, publishers, wholesalers, and distributors.

Most wonderful of all, it gives readers a point-of-purchase at the very moment they first hear about a book that is of interest.

Of course technology in itself is not enough. Publishing success today depends, as it always has, on good writing and good business skills. Writers can write for their own pleasure, but publishers must please the paying public and turn a profit. This doesn't change when writer and publisher are one.

What *has* changed is the variety of options available. Today, trade publishing is just one way to get a manuscript into print. Bookstore distribution is just one way to reach readers. Amazon KDP is just one way to self-publish.

Variety and choice create their own challenges, but as Self-Publishing 3.0 unfolds, authors are working within a more open, equal, and merit-based publishing system than ever before.

Traditionally, the few publishing slots available to authors meant that the majority of aspiring authors were offered scant opportunity.

While individuals working in publishing are caring booklovers who value and honor authors, as we'll see in Chapter 3, the system itself is indifferent, even harsh to most writers. Disrespectful language like "slush pile" is used to describe manuscripts sent in by authors. Contracts license a wide sweep of rights without any clear plan to exploit them. Signed authors are given only token input into key decisions about cover design, positioning, and placement of their books in the marketplace. A long and convoluted supply chain sees authors paid last and given the smallest percentage of everybody involved. Income and royalty statements are all but unreadable.

The inequality baked into traditional publishing arrangements has been revealed by Rebecca Giblin and Joshua Yuvaraj's exploratory study of publishing contracts.[1] This research, sourced from the archive of the Australian Society of Authors, identified "serious deficiencies" in publishing contracts.

> Many contracts were inconsistent or otherwise poorly drafted, key terms were commonly missing altogether, and…critical [author protection] terms evolved very slowly.

In the past, the power dynamics underwriting publishing left authors with no alternative but to accept poor terms and treatment. Writers welcomed the expression of interest and investment that a publishing contract represented. Desperate to be published, they were grateful to those who made it possible, even if conditions were less than ideal.

Successful self-publishing creates a new way of thinking, working, and earning as an author. Many authors are happily making that shift, but others are struggling and not without reason. There are many challenges, none insurmountable, but all requiring time and thought.

I've covered the mental, emotional, and creative shifts needed to embrace the potential of self-publishing today in *Creative Self-Publishing*. Here in this short campaign booklet, my focus is on the historical development of self-publishing, the choices authors are making that are driving this new era of digital creative business for authors, and its potential impact on author earnings and empowerment.

There is widespread misunderstanding of self-publishing, both inside and outside the literary world. Most people speak of two supposedly oppositional pathways to publication: self-publishing (through non-curating platforms like Amazon) and trade-publishing (through curating third-party publishers). They assume that self-publishing is invariably a second-best choice for those who couldn't win a traditional contract. They either don't know or don't understand just how many authors are displaying phenomenal success as publishers.

Yes, only a tiny (and dwindling) proportion of writers with a raw manuscript are going to receive a decent trade-publishing deal. Publishers and agents are now spending more time scouring the bestseller lists looking for authors with a proven self-publishing record than on the "slush pile" of raw manuscripts. And only a tiny proportion of those who do receive a a trade deal go on to have long-term careers with that publisher. But that is of no concern to the dedicated indie author, who has a wide and growing variety of publishing options at home and across the world.

Successful indie authors are selling books through their own websites as well as making them widely available on other online retailers. They may work with trade publishers and other right licensors for some titles while retaining others for themselves. They write under many different pen names and author brands and are inventing new publishing genres, niches, and micro-niches. They are producing a variety of products, in addition to books, and working from a variety of business models.

Observing these pioneers in action, and their commercial and creative achievements, more and more authors are turning to self-publishing, earning how to write and publish well, and succeeding in great number. This has created a benign circle for the enterprising author. As the community gains confidence, strength, and skills through working together for each other's success, more opportunities open up.

This is a story you may entirely miss if you rely on reports from traditional media and publishing bodies.

Author Income and Impact

Anyone who sets out to research the topic of author income will soon find themselves lost in a forest of doom-and-gloom headlines. When the Writers' Union of Canada surveyed its members in 2018, they found what they called "the average writer" made 27% less CAD$ a year from their writing than three years previously, and 78% less than they made in 1998[2].

A 2018 New Zealand survey found that writers earned less than NZ$12,500 from their writing[3], leading New Zealand Society of Authors president Kyle Mewburn to conclude that "the vast majority of writers are working at a minimum wage job with no insurance, overtime or holiday pay, and absolutely no job security. We really need our local readers to buy more local books from local bricks-and-mortar bookshops. Let's just consider it an investment in our cultural health."

A UK income research survey commissioned by the Authors' Licensing and Collecting Society[4] in the same year found average author earnings had fallen by 15% since its previous review in 2013. Another survey by the Arts Council of England[5] looked specifically at fiction. Surveying 10,000 bestselling fiction titles over the previous five years, it concluded that "outside of the top 1,000 authors (at most), printed book sales alone simply cannot provide a decent income...a source of deep concern."

Its solution? More and better grants for authors.

The Arts Council's and author associations' concern is shared by ALLi, but the proposed solutions are not. Even the most generous author grant is paltry when held against the average living wage. Grants take a lot of energy to win and, while they may an invaluable help at a particular point in time for a particular writer, they have a limited time span, are in the form of a gift, and are only available to a certain kind of book and author.

Grants are not the solution to author poverty. Neither is telling readers where they should buy their books. We simply don't have the right to do this, and readers are unlikely to heed such paternalistic injunctions. The solution to author poverty is already up and running, being led by authors themselves.

Developing a sustainable, scalable self-publishing business is the best way for today's author to earn more income, influence, and impact. Encouraging this trend with publishing and author business skills training is the best way for author associations and other concerned bodies to support today's author.

Self-publishing has grown the book market and the number of authors who are earning a living from writing books. This is true whether we look at individual territories like the United States, where self-publishing is most established, or beyond the Western world toward emerging global economies. Traditionally published authors may be suffering falling revenue, but the self-publishing sector is thriving, growing fast according to every metric, including author income.

The phenomenon is being missed by research into author income, partly because it is difficult to track with traditional analytics tools like ISBNs, which only capture a portion of the self-publishing market. Publishing analysts focus on the activity of large publishing conglomerates and tech giants, such as Penguin Random House or Amazon, rather than the micro-businesses of hundreds of thousands of publishing authors.

Literature organizations still think of authorship as an art or a profession and either accidentally or deliberately overlook the growing band of self-publishing authors who are achieving commercial and creative success.

Self-publishing authors now account for 24 to 34% of all e-book sales in each of the largest English-language markets. And one-third of the bestsellers on most publishing platforms are author-published.

Currently, almost 10% of ALLi's membership is in our vetted Authorpreneur Membership category. Authorpreneur members of ALLi have to have sold 50,000 books, or a business equivalent, in the two years before joining. This is a very significant commercial achievement for any publisher, never mind a sole-trader creative business.

Digital author-publishing has only been with us for a decade. Already, by working through companies like Amazon KDP, Apple Books, Google Play, Kobo Writing Life, IngramSpark and many other services around the globe, as well as selling books directly to readers on their own websites, authors are producing more books, earning more revenue, and reaching more readers than all the trade-publishing companies combined[6].

As with all research, it is essential to look closely at the respondents to these author organization surveys and the attitudes that underlie these studies. Such scrutiny reveals that the bodies commissioning the income surveys are largely living in the past, looking at economic models that are no longer dominant, and sharing an assumption that authors are powerless, with their income controlled by external forces.

In the Canadian survey of 1,499 respondents, for example, 20% of the survey group were aged 50 to 60, 62% were aged 60 to 70, and 31% were over the age of 70. The other survey samples similarly skewed older.

The conclusions drawn from these surveys propose solutions from a particular mindset that is not business-friendly and that has a very large blind spot about self-publishing.

This reluctance to talk business is shared by many authors who define themselves as artists or professionals and don't like to think about the commercial side of life. There is an unexamined assumption that business comes between the author and their readers, and between the author and their own creativity.

If this is true for some, it is by no means true for all. On the contrary. We see daily at ALLi that the authors who are working on their publishing and business skills are the ones who are most connected to their readers, and to their own creative mission, passion, and purpose. Ironically, they are producing far more books than the authors who are chasing those elusive, exclusive publishing deals that will allow them to "just write."

Mainstream Media Reports

Alas, mainstream reporters unthinkingly regurgitate the doom-and-gloom stories generated by the surveys. A 2019 article[7] by the US business magazine *Forbes* declared that "Authors Have Suffered A Drastic Decline In Earnings," raising "serious concerns about the future of American literature." Its source was another one of those association surveys, this time the US Authors' Guild[8], packed with much talk of author poverty and financial pressure, and of the writers of literary fiction who "have been hardest hit" in what is portrayed as a crisis.

In the middle, the article offers a throwaway line about "one exception"—the "self-published authors who saw their book-related income almost double since 2013." The journalist doesn't let that stop the article from reaching an overall conclusion of "median income…that has fallen steadily" to an "historic low"—or stop it from providing an infographic showing how authors find it "increasingly difficult to make it," a pictorial representation of average earnings going down, down, down.

There are many factors leading to this drop in author income, we are told, but the bulk of the article focuses on one: Amazon, a familiar obsession for primarily trade-published author bodies.

"When it comes to self-publishing, Amazon controls 85% of the market and that means that authors in that category must accept the company's terms to get their work published," the article says. This betrays a poor understanding of how self-publishing and author business actually work. Amazon self-publishing divisions—Amazon KDP (print and e-book) and ACX (audio)—do not publish books. They are distributors and retailers for independent authors. The author is the publisher and, as we shall see in Part II, the independent author has many choices and opportunities in addition to Amazon, including selling books on their own websites and through a variety of outlets around the world.

That's not to say that Amazon is anything but a clever business, nor to ignore that there are dangers that authors need to understand in its exclusivity, subscription, and advertising programs—but the article makes no mention at all of its positive impact on author income, which is not so much an oversight as a blind spot.

There is a pattern to media stories about author income research, outlined by publishing commentator and ALLi Advisor Jane Friedman. Whenever a new survey is released,

> *Media coverage claims writers' incomes are plummeting, a few big-name authors come out and try to shame publishers, or even society, for not valuing writers properly. Debate ensues. Then everyone gets back to work—until a new study emerges.*[9]

It's time to change this tired approach and the inaccurate viewpoint of authors-as-victims, which is creatively and commercially impoverishing and demotivating.

Supporting an author's need for publishing and business skills is where arts councils and author associations can be most useful in the Self-Publishing 3.0 era, but few literary organizations consider the provision of digital publishing skills, or creative business skills, to fall within their remit. It's time for that, too, to change. Give an author a grant and you feed them for a while. Give them adaptive self-publishing and creative business skills and you feed them for life. The solution to author poverty is author empowerment.

Of course, self-publishing is challenging and doesn't guarantee anyone an income. Of course many beginning authors underestimate what it takes to write and publish well. But what self-publishing does deliver is opportunity. It's still not a perfect world and author-publishing will always be a deeply demanding job. But the digital publishing tools, inexpensive production costs, and global audiences delivered by the Self-Publishing 3.0 era give far more authors far more opportunities for commercial success than ever before.

CHAPTER 2
THE ROAD TO SELF-PUBLISHING 3.0

To fully appreciate the opportunities of the Self-Publishing 3.0 era, it helps to understand how we got here and how authors operate within the current publishing and self-publishing framework. Let's take a spin through the history of self-publishing.

The first crack in the closed publishing system that required expensive publishing presses and access to bookshop distribution came at the end of the twentieth century, when new computer technology facilitated **desktop publishing**. This allowed the creation of print books using page layout software on a personal computer and printer.

Now it was economically viable to print single copies or small book batches to order. Enterprising pioneer authors were soon buying "desktop" computers and printers to run off copies of their books and pamphlets and sell by mail order.

American author Dan Poynter launched a term for this new trend when he wrote (and desktop-published) *The Self-Publishing Manual* in 1979. **Self-Publishing 1.0** had arrived.

SELF-PUBLISHING 1.0

The consumer DTP market exploded in 1985 with the Apple LaserWriter. Other companies got involved, unleashing a wave of author and indie publications, both books and magazines, with indie presses supporting the social movements of the time, like the feminist, gay liberation, and self-help movements.

Lots of novelists and nonfiction authors also took to desktop publishing with gusto. US company Ingram launched Lightning Source as a printer and distributor of what became known as POD books.

Self-Publishing 1.0 wasn't just about print. The idea of e-books had been around as long as mass-market paperbacks, first surfacing in the 1930s, when, after watching his first "talkie" (movie with sound), writer and impresario Bob Brown became obsessed with what he called the "readie"[1]—"a simple reading machine which I can carry or move around [and] attach to any old electric light plug."

On 4 July 1971 came the event that launched the ebook, when Michael Hart typed the US Declaration of Independence into his computer and transmitted it to other users on the computer network at the University of Illinois, where he worked.

From this beginning Hart launched Project Gutenberg and then other enterprising authors jumped in, producing "electronic books" on their websites for sale to readers. Again, adoption was low. The average reader of fiction or poetry didn't delight in reading on a computer and was wary of online commerce.

It wasn't until 1998, twenty-seven years after the launch of Project Gutenberg, that the first e-book retailers and publishers began to emerge.

All in all, it was difficult for authors to make the finances work in the Self-Publishing 1.0 era. Distribution was a major, time-intensive challenge, and bookstores and reviewers refused to engage with self-published books. While some, especially nonfiction authors, set up successful businesses around desktop publishing and POD, most steered clear, preferring to focus on writing and let somebody else look after publishing.

But then came the e-book reader, the Kindle, and KDP publishing.

SELF-PUBLISHING 2.0

Self-publishing 2.0 arrived with mass-market "e-paper technology." Sony released the first e-book reader in 2004, but it was Amazon's Kindle, in 2007, that was the real game changer. Back then, Amazon was already on its way to becoming the biggest online store in the world. The company had begun with books, and when it turned to e-books, it was in the unique position of having this vast online bookstore attached.

E-books could now be easily purchased on a Kindle reader and instantly delivered, using the same log-in used to do your other shopping. But the real innovation, from an author's and publisher's perspective, was the publishing platform that also came attached: Kindle Direct Publishing (KDP).

KDP was not a publisher but a publishing platform. Rights, the font of income for publishers, remained with the rights owner, which, unless a work had been previously licensed, was the author. As there was no rights licensing, there were no royalties or advances on royalties. No money would exchange hands until a book was bought or read by a reader, then KDP would take a commission on each sale (confusingly dubbed a "royalty" by Amazon and some other platforms).

It was an instant switch from a scarcity to an abundance economy. Agents' and publishers' roles as curators and gatekeepers were toppled, and readers would now be the arbiters of a book's success. A computer algorithm would order the rankings, and books that didn't earn reader attention and purchasing would fall away unnoticed.

As well as KDP, Amazon also launched ACX, Audiobook Creation Exchange, as a platform for audiobook production and bought CreateSpace (now KDP Print) for print book production. The company had direct input into all book formats and was ideally primed for speedy growth and dominance of the book business.

Apple iBooks, Barnes & Noble's Nook, Kobo, IngramSpark, and Google Play also came into the marketplace around this time. Like Amazon, none of these invested in the publishing process as a trade publisher would—but neither were they licensing any intellectual property.

Services emerged to aggregate access to self-publishing platforms in one convenient place for authors. Companies like Smashwords, Draft2Digital, PublishDrive, and StreetLib gave authors a one-stop platform with global reach.

Self-Publishing 2.0 changed everything overnight for authors. The combined effect of e-books, online bookstores, and author empowerment turned publishing on its head. Retaining all publishing rights, authors could now reach their readers directly, or through an online retailer, in three formats—audio (a-book), electronic text (e-book), and print (p-book)—and market their book through social media and book influencers like bloggers, reviewers, and, increasingly, libraries.

Some authors set up exclusively on Amazon, but the more business-minded authors embraced nonexclusivity and the freedom to self-publish on many platforms. Emerging at the same time were social networking tools like Facebook, Twitter, Goodreads, Wattpad, and open-source software like WordPress that made website building cheap and easy.

The way was set, and authors took to it in droves.

By the time of Hart's death in 2011, Project Gutenberg hosted e-books in 60 different languages, and authors around the world were making, publishing, and promoting e-books through a variety of retailers.

Publishing has witnessed intense arguments over the merits or otherwise of Amazon, DRM, Internet piracy, POD quality, and many other topics, but everyone involved in self-publishing is agreed that there has never been a better time to be an author.

This is true, but it's important to note just how low the bar has been for most authors, who, in the supply-and-demand scarcity economics of traditional publishing, were dispensable and replaceable.

Most authors didn't get published at all. Even when they did, most of them were dropped after a book or two if sales didn't happen. Even when not dropped, unless they were one of the top 10 sellers, they received little marketing energy or budget. The system created a few stars and vast swathes of losers.

While the Self-Publishing 2.0 era has definitely opened up unprecedented opportunities, authors remain vulnerable. Content is still largely mediated by large corporations: Silicon Valley companies like

Amazon, Apple, and Google these days, rather than Manhattan and London trade publishers, but no less self-interested.

Digital publishing has brought new challenges. Copyright law—the foundation on which author independence and income have traditionally rested—feels unequal to a digital landscape powered by artificial intelligence. The market is hugely imbalanced, with so many "independent" authors tied into an exclusive arrangement with a single distributor-retailer (Amazon KDP).

Subscription reading models offered by Amazon and Spotify, to mention only the two biggest players, look set to further reduce income for authors who focus exclusively on book sales.

Forward-thinking authors understand the implications of this and that the game is changing again. That the author in an exclusive arrangement with Amazon is no more independent than an author in an exclusive arrangement with a trade publisher. That true independence is commercial as well as creative, and that authors who want to succeed today need to learn the art and craft of author-publishing: producing books not just for pleasure but also for profit.

These enterprising, entrepreneurial authors are unfolding Self-Publishing 3.0.

CHAPTER 3
SELF-PUBLISHING 3.0

The foundation of Self-Publishing 3.0 is the understanding that authors today are creative business owners building independent publishing enterprises.

In the past, authors depended for success on influencers and gatekeepers: publishers, agents, librarians, booksellers, professional critics, and reviewers. That system is still in place, though shrinking in size. Today's indie author depends on attracting, engaging, and delighting readers through a variety of platforms and formats and high-level publishing skills. That system is expanding in size and influence, not least on social media, where book content can be repurposed for marketing and author platform building.

In author circles, the larger percentage retained by the self-publishing author receives a lot of attention and is often cited as the primary reason to self-publish. Less discussed, but actually more significant across the long term, is that self-publishing allows an author to publish without having to license their IP.

As a self-publisher, an author retains all rights. This has enormous value which can be assigned... but should never be given away without a decent reward and as part of a wider publishing strategy.

Self-Publishing 3.0 is powered by the **principle of inclusivity:** publishing through as wide a variety of outlets, formats and territories as possible, for maximum visibility and discoverability. **Exclusivity,** by contrast, is confining yourself to one outlet or one format (ebooks, print, audio).

In trade publishing, the default option is exclusivity. Though a publisher might put a book out in multiple outlets, formats or territories, from a contractual perspective, the contract is exclusive. The author cannot publish anywhere outside the bounds of the contract, including their own website.

This is as it needs to be. A publisher investing in a book needs to know that a competing book by another publisher is not going to pop up and cannibalize sales.

Exclusivity in publishing may also refer to distribution in just one region for print books—distribution only in the United States, or the United Kingdom and Commonwealth. Such deals for print books are how trade publishing traditionally protected its investment, as the gentlemen of the "gentleman's profession" divided the English-speaking world between them, agreeing not to publish into each other's territories.

With some exceptions, that system worked for most of the 20th century but the dawn of digital has made it far less workable. Publishers now increasingly seeking world rights for print, as well as ebooks, without paying more for the privilege.

By contrast, self-publishing agreements with online retailers like Amazon KDP, Apple Books, Google Play, IngramSpark and aggregators like Draft2Digital, PublishWide and StreetLib are **inclusive (non-exclusive) by default.** The author is the IP holder, retaining all rights. The services are business partners distributing and, in some cases, retailing the book, and taking a commission from each sale.

Notably Amazon offers **exclusivity programs** that give bonuses and benefits, through **Kindle Direct Publishing Select** (e-book) and **ACX exclusivity option** (audiobooks). Such benefits include higher royalty rates, inclusion in subscription programs, and other marketing tools.

Exclusivity can sometimes encourage other distributors to help with promotion of the book—though not always directly, or on demand. If a book is available exclusively through a specific vendor, and it shows signs of doing well (lots of readers picking it up, reviewing it, etc.), authors may get a friendly and helpful boost from that vendor. They may find their book listed in a promotional email, or placed in a prominent position on a results page.

Advantages of Inclusive Independence

Indie authors love Amazon because its trifecta of digital publishing platform, Kindle reader, and online retail store has allowed so many authors to make a living online. It has been the main engine of the self-publishing revolution to date.

But authors are also aware of the difficulties of dependency. They can feel powerless in their relationship with the tech giant, and feel they have little choice but to do what that company wants in order to continue working with them. That's business, says Amazon.

Yes, it is possible to sell books and make a good income from Amazon only, and the service has a number of excellent promotional tools, but in our estimation none of this outweighs the dangers of exclusivity. At ALLi, we see every week how Kindle Unlimited is a boon to many authors, but also can hurt other authors. We've seen authors' income plummet, or even dry up, without apparent cause. We've seen accounts closed, without explanation. Every time Amazon changes its rules, or algorithms, or releases a new service, a number of Amazon-exclusive authors find their livelihoods devastated.

We've also, since the arrival of Amazon advertising, seen authors spending increasing amounts of money on advertising to maintain their page reads in KU while relying on bonuses from Amazon to make it worthwhile. This is a very dependent business model.

There are other business reasons to publish wide. While Amazon may be the biggest player in the US and the UK, there are other retail stores and devices that dominate in other English-speaking countries, and many other countries outside of the Anglo-American world where books in English are sold.

- At time of writing, Amazon is only active in 13 countries in the world and only 10 of those are eligible for Prime. Apple is in 52 countries, Google Play in 110. Kobo has expanded into more than 70 countries, and sales in Canada come mostly from Kobo for most of

ALLi's members. US and UK centric authors over-estimate Amazon's global dominance because it is the dominant player in those two territories. But 95% of the world, and some important publishing territories, don't have Amazon dominance.

- In Germany, which many experts agree is the next big market for e-books, Amazon has 40% of the market. Apple Books and Tolino (an e-book reader and associated stores run by a group of German publishers) have the rest.
- The biggest book fair in the world take places in Cairo, Egypt. In 2019, it saw over four million visitors pass through its doors (160 times more than the London Book Fair and 13 times more than the Frankfurt Book Fair).

A number of ALLi authorpreneur members are now finding that their growth on vendors outside of Amazon is faster than their growth on Amazon. The author who remains exclusive to Amazon closing off many sales channels and avenues for discoverability. These nascent markets are growing faster than the UK and US markets, which are now mature.

Certainly, an author who is Amazon exclusive is reducing their visibility and discoverability around the world—and in territories and on platforms where it is easier to find a foothold.

Even within the US and UK, the exclusive author is missing out. Just as some readers prefer audio or print to e-books, some are loyal to their Nook (Barnes & Noble), Kobo ereaders, or Apple device and the ease of their associated apps. They cannot read the Amazon-exclusive author in the way they prefer.

Relying solely on one outlet for your business income is risky. It limits options if a particular vendor decides to change the rules. Any perks or benefits that a distributor offers for exclusivity are always at the vendor's discretion. And just as authors will make decisions in the best interest of their business (as they should), a vendor will do the same. Many times those decisions are not favorable to an individual author.

If authors are distributing on a wide model, and particularly if they also sell directly on their own website, these problems are mitigated. They will be able to shift focus away from a dud distribution channel and focus on one that brings greater margins. They will be safe from closures and rule changes and dropped regions because they will have multiple channels where they can aim their efforts.

Yes, it can take longer to become profitable on a range of smaller outlets than one large one. Building a readership always takes time and effort, and exclusivity models, especially at Amazon, offer some shortcuts and promotional opportunities, such as paid page reads and site promotions. In short, by eschewing exclusivity, you build a successful author business just as anybody builds any good business: step by step, asset by asset, book by book.

Seven Publishing Options

The principle of inclusivity enables seven publishing choices that make for a sustainable, long-term, scalable income.

1. **Direct sales:** Authors selling books to readers from their own author websites.
2. **Publishing wide:** Authors using a wide variety of platforms and retailers to globally sell their books to readers in the widest possible variety of formats—e-book, audiobook, paperback, hardback, large print, box sets, special editions.
3. **ACCESS Marketing:** Authors gaining access to reader attention and action through social media and direct communications, e.g. emails or texts.
4. **Influencer Marketing:** Authors reaching readers through literary influencers like libraries, reviewers, podcasters, bloggers, and other influential authors.
5. **Author collaboration:** Authors who take their working relationship further, joining together to write, publish, or market books together, to enhance each other's impact, influence, discoverability, reach, and income.
6. **Selective rights licensing:** Authors shunning exclusive publishing and self-publishing deals, instead always limiting the formats, term, and territories licensed to publishers, other rights buyers, and self-publishing services.

7. **Author Special Sales:** Authors publishing and selling print books and other physical products in bulk through non-bookstore, non-traditional marketing.

Self-Publishing 3.0 is already up and running. Authors are already selling directly from their websites, already publishing widely in three digital formats (e-book, print-on-demand, and audiobook), already distributing through an increasing variety of outlets and in a variety of languages across the world, and already selectively licensing non-exclusive rights instead of leaping into the exclusive and binding contracts of old.

Readers are also beginning to appreciate the new publishing landscape, relishing the closer connection with authors, becoming more comfortable with purchasing directly from creators, joining crowd-funders, and signing up as patrons through Patreon and other outlets.

PART II
SELF-PUBLISHING 3.0 DRIVERS

CHAPTER 4
DIRECT SALES

Direct selling is authors selling books to readers from their own author website or app. Direct sales not only bring higher revenue, they allow authors to learn more about their readers, create a closer relationship with them, and strengthen their author platform in numerous ways.

A direct sales strategy means authors stop sending readers to other retailers by default and think of them as services to aid discovery and sales growth. Instead of moving through a chain of distribution and retail intermediaries, all of whom take a cut from the profit on the sale, direct sales allow authors to net the full profit on the book, minus a small transactional fee.

When investing in ads or other kinds of book promotion, the author guides readers to purchase on their own site instead of someone else's. The author pays a small transaction fee to an e-commerce platform, approx 5% per transaction, a lot less than the minimum 30% charged by retailers like Amazon, Kobo, and others, and a further 30% of those net payments charged by aggregators.

This is not a recommendation to take books off such retailers, who make amazing things happen for authors every day. It's not either/or but both.

One of the big advantages of digital bookselling over physical sales is that the reader encounters a buy button just when they are reading about a book and deciding whether they like the sound of it. It's fine for authors who are contractually published to have a brochure site that points elsewhere to buy—they are only receiving a small single-figure percentage of each sale—but indie authors generally find it impossible to build a sustainable business without a transactional website.

A transactional website will also host an author's "traffic generator": a blog, vlog, or podcast that brings readers to their website and encourages traffic that makes them attractive to other authors and influencers. The site can also generate sales coupons and other incentives for targeted book promotions, host crowdfunders, patronage, other special projects, and display social media accounts.

Informing Readers

Most readers are shocked when they discover that when they spend $10 in a bookstore, the author receives less than $1.

Readers think all writers are rich, that if they've heard of the author they must be famous and, by corollary, if they haven't, they're not. They are truly shocked to hear that most writers in the trade-publishing model are earning less than the minimum wage.

They mostly have no idea about how they can support authors in their endeavors, what a difference it makes to authors when they buy directly instead of on another online store, and how much a donation or other form of patronage means to an author's ability to keep going. It is up to authors to inform them.

When readers understand what a difference it makes to authors if they are a patron, what a difference it makes if they buy direct rather than from somebody else, they want to help with that and be part of the publishing adventure.

There are some disadvantages to selling directly from an author website and some key challenges to overcome. The biggest disadvantage is that sales do not count toward any kind of ranking on Amazon or a media bestseller list. In wide circles, this is known as "bank before rank." However, a lot of authors leverage their success in online retailers, as reader-purchase algorithms make them more visible to new readers, especially on Amazon. If you sell most books on your author website, you are accepting that you are unlikely to hit the top of the charts and also that you will lose any advantages of exclusivity.

There are other practical challenges, costs, and responsibilities of owning and maintaining a transactional website, including tax responsibilities and service terms and conditions. So, a transactional website takes more time and thought to set up, yes, but the advantages, in terms of independence, control, and business intelligence, greatly outweigh the disadvantages.

Authors set up for direct sales are also well-prepared for an incoming technology that many feel has the potential to further decentralize publishing: the blockchain. See ALLi's white paper Authors and the Blockchain (*SelfPublishingAdvice.org/blockchain*) for more on this.

For more on direct sales, see **The Ultimate Guide to Selling Books on Your Author Website** *in ALLi's Self-Publishing Advice Center:*
SelfPublishingAdvice.org/directselling

CHAPTER 5
PUBLISHING WIDE
MULTIPLE RETAILERS, REGIONS & FORMATS

To "go wide" or "publish wide" is to distribute and sell books via multiple platforms, uploading directly to platforms such as Kobo or Apple Books or uploading to multiples sites via an aggregator like Draft2Digital, PublishDrive, or StreetLib. Or, most often, both.

As a guiding principle, and recognizing that there are time constraints and other factors at play, ALLi advises authors to go wide—to make their writing available wherever people might find and enjoy it, through as many different retailers, regions, and formats as possible, given their personal limitations of time, money, and other resources.

The principle is that the more retailers, regions, and formats a book is in, the stronger its foundation for consistent, long-term income. This means valuing the principle of **non-exclusivity,** espoused in Chapter 3.

Exclusivity can sometimes encourage a distributor to help with promotion of the book—though not always directly or on demand. If a book is available exclusively through a specific vendor, and it shows signs of doing well (lots of readers picking it up, reviewing it, etc.), authors may get a friendly and helpful boost from that vendor. They may find their book listed in a promotional email or placed in a prominent position on a results page. These sorts of perks may happen anyway, if the book really is doing well, whether authors are wide or exclusive.

In addition to the dangers of exclusivity outlined in Chapter 3, it's worth noting that, from a business perspective, Amazon is the most competitive store. Since the time Amazon Advertising was launched, it is also the one that costs the most to get visibility. While non-Amazon retailers are smaller, it can be much easier to establish a foothold there.

The more outlets an author has, the less dependent they are on any one. ALLi has many, many members who publish wide to just as much success as Amazon-exclusive authors. All of these wide publishers have one thing in common. They understand that being wide is a long-term strategy, and they are committed to it. Building a presence and garnering sales on Apple Books, Barnes & Noble, Kobo, Google Play, and IngramSpark takes time.

Going wide is also more human centred. While Amazon runs on algorithms, the best visibility spots on the other retailers are curated by humans. Only Google Play could be considered as predominantly algorithmic, and there too the best visibility spots there are hand-curated.

Widely published books have a much higher chance than Kindle Unlimited books of being accepted for BookBub featured deals and other promotion services. A single featured deal will skyrocket your sales on all retailers, which will likely get the attention of the merchandising teams, who may in turn feature your book in their promos, thus driving even more sales. This is how presence is built on non-Amazon retailers.

ALLi Recommendations for Publishing Wide

To avail of the best financial return on the widest possible distribution, ALLi recommends that, time permitting, you upload directly to the e-book Big Five—Amazon's KDP, Apple Books, Barnes & Noble's Nook, Google Play, and Kobo Writing Life—and use one or more e-book aggregators to cover the rest of the world.

If you use those five for your e-books, together with Amazon KDPP and IngramSpark for print as described above, and ACX and Findaway

Voices or similar for audio, you have covered the channels that account for 97% of e-book, p-book, and a-book sales around the western world and maximized your income from them.

The benefits of uploading directly to the big retailers include faster payments, up-to-date sales figures (important for measuring the effectiveness of marketing), more direct control of metadata (particularly categories and keywords which are important for discoverability), and the ability to manipulate pricing quickly and easily (important for promotion).

And, of course, aggregators like PublishDrive, Smashwords, Draft2Digital, and Streetlib take their payment on top of that which is paid to the publishing platforms.

"Time permitting" is a key condition for indie authors though. As writers, especially if we have day jobs and other commitments, our writing time must be protected. The drawback to going direct to all five e-book retailers is that each one has different dashboards and requirements so it can be time-consuming, especially if you have a lot of titles.

And not everyone *can* make the choice to go direct. The US and UK are best served, but options vary widely around the world. Apple famously requires self-publishers to use a Mac to upload, and many find it makes more financial sense to use an aggregator, rather than go through the expense of purchasing a Mac or the hassle of borrowing one.

Lots of ALLi members use assistants to do uploads and other admin. If you seek assistance for your distribution tasks, ensure that the dashboards remain in your author name and that the payments go directly to your account, not that of an intermediary service or agent.

Using Aggregators

Whether you use Amazon only or all the Big Five, do use an aggregator distributor, too. They will reach parts of the world you can't reach any other way. Although at the moment, the smaller retailers around the world account for a negligible proportion of sales, they help to increase your visibility and take very little time to set up. They are also growing far more rapidly than the more mature North American, UK, and Australia-New Zealand markets. Having a more global outlook on the publishing world means using wide distribution aggregators like Draft2Digital, PublishDrive, and StreetLib who will put books in thousands of different online stores, libraries, subscription services, and any other place where digital books are sold.

By taking time to choose what is unique among these outlets, authors can reach the largest possible number of stores. Of course, this can make things a bit more complex to manage. If looking for an easy solution, pick the aggregator that has the widest selection of outlets and that continues to explore new markets.

Every aggregator has its own merits and quirks. Draft2Digital is more US-centric, PublishDrive uses a subscription payment model, StreetLib has most global outlets, and IngramSpark allows you to have e-books and print under one roof. Authors should do their research and make the decision that gives them the best balance of reach and time.

Going wide, which includes the author's own website, is ALLi's recommendation for long-term, sustainable, scalable growth, but there is no point in just offering a book on lots of different websites without a robust sales and marketing plan. Distribution without marketing and promotion will take few books anywhere.

For more on this, see *ALLi's Guide to Publishing Wide* (2021) and *Choose the Best Self-Publishing Services: ALLi's Guide to Assembling Your Tools and Your Team* (2020)

CHAPTER 6
ACCESS MARKETING

ACCESS Marketing is the term I use to describe the kind of marketing that aims to get access to readers' direct contact details and—crucially—their permission to contact them. The method has six steps that lead to a book sale, but its most salient feature is there in the name: the reader gives *access*.

For most authors, access takes the form of an email address, but it can also be phone numbers or social media messenger boxes.

After their books, this list of readers' contact details along with permission to contact them directly, is an indie author's most important asset.

ACCESS stands for *attract, captivate, connect, engage, subscribe*, and *satisfy*.

- **Attract**. The author finds readers through social media and advertising activity online—blog, podcast, video, ads—that use carefully chosen words and images designed to hook the right readers. This content is crafted to be unique and remarkable, offering real value that aligns with the value offered in the author's books.
- **Captivate**. The author consistently releases captivating content on a schedule that suits their writing process, keeps existing followers interested, and attracts newcomers.
- **Connect**. The author offers an email address or other channel by

which followers can connect with them and perhaps also with each other.

• **Engage**. The author makes their channel meaningful by starting and nurturing valuable conversations with followers, aligning all the time with the values that attracted them to that channel and with the value offered in the author's books.

• **Subscribe**. The author invites followers to sign up to receive some free content in exchange for their email address or other contact details.

• **Satisfy**. The author values their potential reader's email address and uses it wisely, contacting them regularly to offer more value. Emails to readers match the original attractor content, are exciting and delightful, and immerse them in the world of the author and the books.

Once these ACCESS marketing steps are completed, selling to this group becomes easy. The author is not pushing their work on readers; the readers are asking, "When is the next book out?"

When the time comes, it's just a matter of sending an email or other message about the book and where to purchase. Readers already know, like, and trust the author and the work. They review positively and spread the word because the author has done the work—craft work and emotional labor—that gains precious reader access and loyalty and continues to nurture it.

With this positive relationship in place, the author can also offer followers other premium products and services as well as books.

For more on ACCESS Marketing, see *Reach More Readers, Sell More Books: ALLI's Guide to Book Marketing for Authors and Poets* by Orna A. Ross (2021)

CHAPTER 7
INFLUENCER MARKETING

An influencer is a person with authority and popularity within a specific niche. Influencers have a large or dedicated following who pay attention to what they say, like, and recommend. They have their audience's trust and attention—both currencies that have always been at a premium in the literary world.

The aim of influencer marketing for authors is to identify influencers in your niche and persuade them to promote your book to their followers and fans. A literary or publishing influencer is anyone with a tribe of readers:

- Academic critics
- Bestselling authors in your niche
- Book bloggers
- Bookstores
- Celebrities
- Community leaders
- Educators
- Experts
- Libraries
- Literary magazines
- Newspaper review supplements

- Podcasters
- Pro speakers
- Social media stars
- Reviewers
- University trendsetters
- YouTubers

The list is long, and we can add many more.

The traditional influencers in the book business are booksellers, libraries, reviewers, and critics. Gaining their attention means reviews in the literary and mainstream press. This sort of influencer reaches a wide range of readers across the mainstream book-reading market. Since the advent of digital publishing, this form of influence is waning, and the reach of influencers who are more niche, who target a particular category of readers online, is expanding.

While traditional attention can garner praise and respect for your book, finding those who are most influential with the readers who are most likely to buy, is a better sales strategy. This means knowing your genre, niche, and micro-niche as well as the mediators and other authors who are known, liked, and trusted by your potential readers.

Some authors are becoming influencers themselves, able to attract sponsorship to recommend products to their readers. Influencer marketing works best when the author taps into influencer insights about what makes their audience tick and when the campaign feels meaningful to both, rather than the author–publisher just using the influencer as a passive mode of passing on a marketing message.

For more on influencer marketing see *Reach More Readers, Sell More Books: ALLI's Guide to Book Marketing for Authors and Poets* by Orna A. Ross (2021)

CHAPTER 8
AUTHOR COLLABORATION

ALLi is built on author collaboration. Every day, we witness our members paying forward tips about tech, tricks, and tools, knowledge that gives real competitive advantages to another. Our team and advisors are set up to do precisely that. And the entire self-publishing space is full of entrepreneurial authors openly sharing sales numbers, tools, and techniques and promoting each other through blog posts, podcasts, email lists, and social networks.

We are also increasingly seeing authors enter formal writing and publishing collaborations.

For indie authors publishing digitally in e-book and audio and by print-on-demand, readers are not a finite commodity. Nor are they assets to be kept from other writers. Indie authors know they enjoy a global marketplace so large that no writer will ever reach all the readers out there, while the right kind of author collaboration in writing and publishing greatly increases the odds of getting discovered, noticed, and read.

In traditional, physical bookstore selling, where only a handful of titles can be accommodated, the author space is notoriously competitive. With digital publishing, there's no pressure to sell a certain number of books within the first few months. Traditionally published authors in the past had to compete with each other—for agents, publishing deals, prizes, or cooperation as well as shelf space—but today's indie author has nothing to fear from cooperating with other authors.

When indie authors speak about "author comps," they mean comparable, not competing authors. They enjoy "coopetition" (cooperating with perceived competition so that both parties benefit) and know that, in working and educating together, they learn faster and respond and adapt more nimbly. In short, they do better together than by going it alone.

Author collaborations can be in writing (e.g. creating a book together, creating a shared universe, creating a single pen name that many authors contribute to, creating anthologies) or in publishing (e.g. banding together to make box sets, swap author promotions, put together themed collections, share add space, host takeovers on each other's platforms, and many other options).

When a writing collaboration works, partners inspire and complement one other and the creative process is less lonely. But for every successful writing partnership, there are dozens of failed ones. Having a thorough discussion about hopes and expectations, including the salient details in a collaboration agreement, improve the odds of success.

For author collaboration advice see SelfPublishingAdvice.org/author-collaboration

ALLI members have access to *sample agreements, including collaboration agreement. Log in at* AllianceIndependentAuthors.org *and navigate to contracts, then to sample agreements.*

CHAPTER 9
SELECTIVE RIGHTS LICENSING

While authors tend to focus on book sales as the endgame of the publishing process, each of their books actually represents several sets of rights, each of which should be licensed separately and selectively.

Self-Publishing 3.0 is a way of thinking about publishing that shatters the binary choice between exclusively licensing all publishing rights to one trade (traditional) publisher on the one hand versus exclusively self-publishing on the other. This is most obvious in the arena of rights.

Today, e-book, print book (in different formats like hardback and large print), and audiobook are all formats authors can publish themselves. When it comes to film, international editions, stage adaptations, merchandising, and more, successful authors license rights to other creative companies, services, or individuals. They can work with print publishers, across the world, in the same way.

The publishing industry has been exploiting rights for many years, but indie authors are now starting to trade their own publishing rights in ways that maximize the return on their intellectual property. This is a fantastic benefit—but only if authors are aware of its value and know how to exploit it.

It used to be that authors were so grateful to find a publisher that they would exclusively assign all rights. The confidence instilled in the author community by the experience of self-publishing has made this attitude is less widespread. With such confidence in place, the offer of a trade-publishing deal, or an assisted publishing deal, becomes a different proposition. The author's attitude changes to "What are you, the publishing service, bringing to the table? What do I have to give up? What do I gain?"

Successful independent authors do not see themselves as content providers for the trade-publishing industry. They see a trade publisher as a potential partner. They work with a publisher if the deal is good and makes sense for a particular book, but they license rights *selectively*.

Selective Rights Licensing

Selective rights licensing means that, rather than granting or assigning all the rights in a title to one publisher, authors understand that each right is a separate package that may be separately licensed in exchange for compensation in the form of a flat fee, or royalties, or residuals, or commissions.

Instead of automatically licensing all rights, they offer only the right the publisher is seeking to exploit—the right to produce an audiobook, for example, or to translate the work, or release a print edition in a particular territory—and only when they have a sense of the sales plan for the book. They limit the territory and format and term of the contract as tightly as possible.

As a general rule of thumb, the savvy author attempts to negotiate each sub-right individually, making separate decisions based on market size, the reach of the publisher, and the potential value of the right.

We talk about "selling" rights, but that is not quite accurate. What authors do is license a user—a publisher, a production company, a manufacturer— to exploit a specific right for a specific term and territory, with a clear reversion clause so that, if things go wrong, they can easily extract themselves from the deal.

Without an understanding of copyright, and the ability to license and negotiate publishing rights, authors can be seduced by offers that in reality offer very little. It is common to see contracts granting publishers world English-language rights and all subsidiary rights, including valuable e-book rights, in return for a paltry (or sometimes no) advance and low royalties. Some add the insult of a very long rights term—in extreme cases life of copyright—to the injury of poor terms and conditions.

A great many self-publishing services, many of which are found at the top of internet search listings, also offer problematic contracts. Other dangers are alleged "hybrid" arrangements that are really vanity operations where the author takes all the risk. Or offers from overseas "publishers" in countries that are not covered by copyright agreements, or where piracy is rife, or payment unlikely.

Licenses to publish come in many flavors. They may be exclusive (meaning only the licensee has permission to use the work) or nonexclusive (meaning more than one person may use the work at the same time).

Sometimes subsidiary rights like TV, film and others can be more valuable than the original book rights, so it's important that authors understand the licensing terms being offered.

Understanding and maintaining clear control over rights is a key strategy in an indie author's toolbox.

For more on selective rights licensing see ALLi's guide: How Authors Sell Publishing Rights

ALLi members can get contract and rights advice from a dedicated literary agent. For more information: allianceIndependentAuthors.org/rights

---

CHAPTER 10
AUTHOR SPECIAL SALES

Special sales are physical or digital books or recordings sold in bulk, and non-returnable, to non-bookstore outlets. Readers find the book in places where they buy related items, rather than going to a bookstore to specifically shop for books.

According to the Association for Publishers of Special Sales[1], more than half of all books distributed annually by US publishers are special sales. *Incentive* magazine says books have an approximately 6% share of the "incentive market," worth $1.5 billion in the US alone.

Taking books to readers where they are rather than waiting for them to go to a bookstore is the essence of special sales—where they shop (bookstores, gift shops, catalogs), gather (seminars, libraries, associations) or work (offices, schools, hospitals). The outlets may be retail (discount stores, gift shops, supermarkets, and airport stores) but not necessarily. Non-retail outlets (corporations, associations, foundations, education companies, government agencies, network-marketing organizations, and more) all use books as incentives, as marketing tools, as sales drivers, to help or entertain their communities.

Special sales outlets include, but are not limited to:

- Corporations that gift books to employees, clients, potential clients.

- Educators or coaches who offer books to students, trainees, or seminar attendees.
- Nonprofit organizations that give books to donors to thank and honor their contributions.
- Associations, hospitals, universities, schools, gift shops, and museum stores.

There are also **special distribution channels** that purchase books for resale in bulk, similar to how publishers market print books to bookstores: from publisher distribution partner to retailer to reader. What is different is that the author directly contacts, negotiates with, ships to, and bills the organization's representative on a sale-without-return basis in exchange for a deep discount.

The special sales process calls on author–publishers to think creatively about how to sell their books, and it's not for every author. It requires an understanding of successful selling techniques, cold pitching, patience (it can take as much as a year to reach a deal), and the ability to accept rejection without becoming derailed.

For many indie authors, this sort of selling is exactly what they want to avoid by self-publishing. But for those who enjoy this sort of direct contact, the rewards are considerable when one customer buys tens of thousands of nonreturnable physical books and expands their reach and word-of-mouth.

For more on special sales for authors see SelfPublishingAdvice.org/specialsales

PART III
SELF-PUBLISHING 3.0 IN PRACTICE

CHAPTER 11
DEVELOPING A FAN BASE

Armed with the techniques outlined in Part II, independent authors in the Self-Publishing 3.0 era see themselves as the creative directors of their books, from concept to completion and beyond.

They work with platforms and services that deliver the best possible books to the most possible readers. In conversations or negotiations with trade publishers and other rights buyers, they employ a selective rights licensing approach. They have, or are working toward having, a website as the hub of their author business, and it is transactional so they can sell directly to readers. They know how to attract, captivate, engage, and sell to the right readers of their books. They may employ special sales.

Whatever avenues they pursue, they collaborate with other authors to mutual benefit as much as possible.

The other part of successful creative business for some authors is exploiting opportunities beyond the book.

A successful business owner either sells a lot of low-priced product or fewer high-priced products, or some mix of the two. Authors today can choose from a variety of business model to employ the one that best suits their creative intentions and conditions and personal preferences.

Earning a full-time living from book sales alone has always been rare, particularly in certain genres like literary fiction and poetry. That has changed with the global audience now available through digital publishing. In theory, every genre now has enough readers to support a business. In practice, finding enough readers and selling enough books is still easiest in genres that attract what are known in the business as "whale readers" (see below), readers who consume books at a fast pace.

For authors in less consumption-driven genres, setting up for success often means seeing your books as part of a bigger picture. In business terms, this means considering the business model *around* your books.

Such authors develop premium products and services and other income streams to supplement book income.

These authors can't, or don't want to, rely on books alone to build a profitable business from their words. Perhaps they don't publish books frequently enough. Or they are in a low-selling genre. Or they prefer more profitable sales margins than books, which are very low-margin. Books take a long time to create and are underpriced compared with other forms of entertainment, education, and inspiration. Creating a sustainable, scalable author business is made easier by incorporating other products, projects, services, and earning strategies into a publishing business.

A variety of products and income streams can expand and deepen the mission, passion, and purpose that fires your books.

The concept of the true fan was originally proposed in 2007 by Kevin Kelly, founder of *Wired* magazine, in an influential article, "1,000 True Fans," which predicted that the internet would allow writers and other creators to make a living from their creative work. Rather than pursuing widespread celebrity, he argued, creators only needed to engage a modest base of "true fans" who will "buy anything you produce" to the tune of $100 per fan, per year. That gives a total annual income of $100,000.

Today, with the creator economy in the midst of a shift from a "bigger is better," ad-driven revenue model to one of niche communities and direct user-to-creator payments, the concept has been updated (with Kelly's blessing) by Li Jin[1], an expert in the emerging "passion economy," to even fewer and truer fans: 100 or so fans, paying approximately $1000 a year.

On Patreon, the average initial pledge amount has increased 22 percent over the past two years. Since 2017, the share of new patrons paying more than $100 per month—or $1,200 per year—has grown 21 percent. On the online course platform Podia, the number of creators earning more than $1,000 in a month is growing 20 percent each month, while the average number of customers per creator is growing at a rate of 10 percent. Likewise, on Teachable, the average price point per class offering has risen roughly 20 percent, year over year. In 2019, nearly 500 Teachable course creators made more than $100,000; of those, 25 averaged more than $1,000 per sale.

Instead of trying to reach hundreds of thousands of readers, the intent is to more deeply satisfy a smaller group of true fans.

In addition to books in print, e-book, audiobook, large print, and workbook editions, your website might offer:

- A **teaching** platform for courses.
- A **coaching** or **consultancy** hub.
- A place to attract clients for **freelance** work.
- A place to offer, and take payment for, other **services**, **tools**, or **products** that have nothing to do with the books.
- A **membership** website that offers a premium product or experience to close readers.
- A place to recommend other services, tools, or products that can bring in **affiliate** income.
- A **donate** button and encouragement for readers to express appreciation through donation.
- Any other **creative offerings** authors can think of that further their influence, impact, mission, and passion that readers would love.

This is different from being a freelancer or employee, which is doing work for others to meet the bills. This is integrating activities that support your mission as a writer and your passion as a person into your author business.

For the entrepreneurial author, this offers a real alternative to taking a day job. For the fully fledged authorpreneur, it offers a higher return and expanded reach, growing income and influence, while simultaneously feeding into book production and sales.

Let's look more closely at possible business models for authors.

CHAPTER 12
BUSINESS MODELS FOR AUTHORS
THINKING BEYOND THE BOOK

The following business models are those most widely used by ALLi members. To run many of these business models, you need a transactional website: not just a brochure site that shows books, but a shop where readers can buy books and other products directly from you.

Model 1: Book Sales Only, One Outlet: Write Fast, Publish Often

This is probably the most visible publishing model in the self-publishing community through Amazon's bestseller lists and promotion engines. And a number of vocal authors who run this model also run courses or write books about how to do it. Authors employing this business model are Amazon KDP authors, often in the exclusive KU arrangement, writing in a popular genre, publishing fast and often, and always with a close eye on the Amazon algorithm.

Some authors employing this model publish only in e-book and do not buy their own ISBNs.

This model has delivered excellent sales for authors in fiction genres like romance, crime, and science fiction/fantasy; nonfiction genres like self-help and business books; and poetry genres like romance, self-help and inspirational poetry. Writers who do well in these genres can sometimes find it impossible to keep up with their readers, which is why a number of authors in these genres are now commissioning other authors to write in their fictional world or for their publishing companies.

The advantage of this model is its simplicity. You can focus just on writing books, the marketing methods that send a book up the charts on Amazon, and harnessing the power of the Amazon algorithm to find new readers. But it is actually a risky business model. A self-publishing author bound exclusively to one distribution outlet is as vulnerable as an author exclusively bound to a single trade publisher. Authors can suffer badly when their only outlet changes terms and conditions in unfavorable ways.

The advantages of exclusivity over its disadvantages have to be carefully weighed, taking a long-term as well as a short-term viewpoint. That said, the single outlet model with Amazon KDP has been incredibly positive for many indie authors.

Model 2: Book Sales Only, Going Wide: Multiple Formats, Multiple Retailers

As we've seen, the indie author community refers to this model as "going wide," meaning publishing directly through a variety of distributors such as Apple Books, Google Play, IngramSpark, and Kobo in addition to Amazon KDP and ACX, as well as aggregator distributors like Draft2Digital, PublishDrive, and StreetLib.

Authors using this model aim is to reach as many readers as possible by being available not just through as many distributors as possible, but also in as many formats as possible and across as many territories as possible.

The advantage of this model is its diversity and consequent stability.

Model 3: Book Sales Plus Speaking or Performance

Publishing books plus speaking or performance is a model often used by nonfiction writers and poets, whereby books are supplemented by speaker income and live events. Offline, this is done as book sales at a paid gig. Online, video performances or webinars lead people to buy books and/or higher-margin products (often called "courses"), often supplemented by an online closed forum.

Model 4: Book Sales Plus Teaching: Supported Learning

Active teaching in a supported-learning environment differs from the previous model (information products/content) because it involves the author (and/or their team) setting exercises, correcting modules, and giving individual feedback within a supported pedagogic structure, as opposed to an information product plus online group.

The time-honored way is through an educational establishment, like a university or school, but now it happens online too, in the form of courses as well as mentoring, coaching, and consultancy.

Model 5: Book Sales Plus Affiliate Income

Under this model, authors supplement their book income with publishing services to other authors. This model often includes recommending to their readership products and services they have used and believe in. The products are often linked to the author's subject matter, theme, or world, and the author promotes them through blog posts, articles, videos, and podcasts with affiliate links to the products.

Model 6: Book Sales Plus Articles, Poems, or Short Stories

Independent authors using this model are not those who use freelance journalism or copywriting income, like a day job, to supplement their book sales. This business model for indie authors is publishing shorter articles, poems, and stories for payment yes, but in ways that complement and enhance their existing author business and books.

They may be paid by traditional media outlets like newspapers or magazines or new media crowdsourced payment sites, or they may run the publications for payment on their own websites or patron sites. The latter version of this model requires a high-traffic website.

Model 7: Membership Model: Benefits for Close Readers

In this model, authors invite keen readers to subscribe monthly or annually to a membership program that offers various benefits. This model often works better for nonfiction, although some fiction authors and poets are achieving great success.

There are four types of membership model: how-to, motivation and accountability, community, and access.

- The how-to membership sites solve a distinct problem, e.g. how to play guitar or how to run a business.
- Motivational memberships offer encouragement and support toward achieving a goal. Members share their struggles and successes and hold each other accountable.
- Connector membership, also known as community memberships, offers people a place to connect and belong. Members are united around a common cause or life experience which the author writes about.
- Access memberships are for fans who want more of the author who may offer online chats, Ask Me Anythings, and do some on-the-spot writing or reading.

Model 8: Influencer Income: Sponsorship or Advertising

Some authors have a following that is attractive to brands which sponsor an aspect of an author's work in return for exposure to the author's followers and fans. Individual books can be sponsored or carry advertising, but that is far less common than sponsorship for some other aspect of the author's work, e.g. YouTube channel or podcast or advertising in a magazine.

Model 9: Book Sales Plus Patronage and Grants

Many literary novels and deeply researched nonfiction books begin with a thank-you to a grant body or award that "made the book possible." A grant can be a boon to a writer, and there are many stories from the 19th and early 20th century of writers who could not have kept going without their benefactors, e.g. WB Yeats and Lady Gregory, James Joyce and Sylvia Beach.

However, wealthy patrons have never been as generous to writers as they have been to visual artists. Around the mid-20th century the professional author was more likely to find support from the arts council or a literary organization which offered various endowments and awards.

Most patronage these days comes from readers, whether through direct donations on authors' websites or through Patreon or similar platforms.

Model 10: Book Sales Plus Rights Licensing or Merchandising

Independent authors are selectively licensing some of their rights to publishing partners, rights buyers, and licensing operators in their home territories and abroad. Publishing rights include print and other rights to English-language publishers, translations, audiobooks, TV/film/documentary, among others. In some cases, authors are also mining their own merchandising, translation, and multimedia rights.

This model generally requires the author to have already had significant success in book sales for other rights buyers to be interested, though occasionally rights are sold on the merit of the idea, book proposal, or book.

Model 11: Book Sales Plus Author Services

In this model, the author combines their own writing and publishing with a product or service based around one of the seven processes of publishing: editing, design, production, distribution, marketing, promotion, or rights licensing.

Model 12: Multiple Streams of income

It is possible to combine a number of these models and enjoy multiple streams of income in addition to book sales. Best results are had when the other projects and products in the business mirror the same mission and passion that inspire the books, and the author has an ecosystem of products, including gift products, free reader-attraction products, core products (books), and premium products.

Whichever model authors use, the benefit of being an independent author is getting to choose how they run their business. If something doesn't work, they get to change it.

These 12 business models for indie authors represent what's working now, but with our changeable industry, the future might hold 12 more possibilities.

The Challenges

So yes, digital publishing affords the indie author a variety of means to build a business, step by step, sale by sale, asset by asset—just as any other business must grow.

Of course, this is easier said than done. Becoming a good enough writer, good enough publisher, and good enough business owner to see sustainable success means learning a lot of new activities all together, and it can quickly become overwhelming.

There are a number of key challenges that every author must overcome in order to establish a profitable author business, including but not limited to:

Writing with skill and flair: A perennial challenge that often gets forgotten in publishing conversations. Depending on genre, it can take years to become skilled enough to offer real value to readers.

Publishing with skill and flair: Turning manuscripts into high-quality, commercially viable books that equal or exceed industry standards, and then, through great book and author branding and sharply honed marketing and promotion, selling sufficient numbers of them to turn a profit.

Running a creative business with skill and flair: Managing the resources and processes, tools and teams that create great books and reach sufficient numbers of readers.

Building a team: Though it's called *self*-publishing, authors work with other publishing professionals to create good books and reach the right readers. Finding the right people and building a team of good editors, designers, and other assistants takes time and people skills.

Encouraging critique: When authors hire their own editors, designers, and production people, they may not be challenged enough by those around them. The indie author needs to be mature enough to be open to constructive feedback, whether positive or negative, and to manage the emotions that may rise in response. Both positive and negative feedback can be emotionally derailing for a creative. The optimal response is one of equanimous exploration in a spirit of learning. The successful self-publisher develops coping mechanisms that remove personal feelings from the act of receiving and accepting criticism, so it can be creatively integrated into their process.

Finding acceptance, validation, or kudos: While things have improved (see Open Up To Indie Authors #PublishingOpenUp), much of the wider literary and publishing world (e.g. bookstores, literary festivals, and prestigious prizes and awards) are still closed to indie authors.

Embracing change: Many authors consciously or unconsciously carry outdated definitions of authorship and success.

Valuing our work: Many authors are suspicious of money, capitalism, and finance systems while bemoaning poverty, needing to make a living, and trying to run an author business. So many authors give away work for free without a clear strategy or for too low a price to make a profit. Few have a solid plan for sales, income, expenses, salary, and profits. Many sign up to schemes and scams that exploit their dreams. Few engage with the contracts and agreements they sign. Many overvalue their work emotionally while undervaluing it commercially.

The publishing industry has taken advantage of these tendencies. And for centuries, authors have been at the rough end of a power imbalance. Now that the bookselling system that kept this inequality in place has been prised open, can authors step forward in sufficient numbers and do the work that will bring about true transformation?

That more than any other single factor will determine whether the promise of the Self-Publishing 3.0 era is fulfilled.

CHAPTER 13

AUTHOR EMPOWERMENT

So, Self-Publishing 3.0 offers an exciting collective challenge to authors. The more indie authors do well—build successful businesses, insist on non-exclusivity, connect directly with readers, selectively license rights, collaborate together—the more influence and impact they have on other writers, on readers, on publishing partners, and on society at large.

It's quite a journey, though, from aspiring author to creative director of an author enterprise, and it requires quite a mental, emotional, and practical shift and takes the writer on a steep learning curve. To make the necessary shifts, many authors need support—but as I write (at the beginning of 2021), the literary, publishing, and industry bodies responsible for creative business, entrepreneurship, culture, and intellectual property have not yet tuned into the needs and influence of the self-publishing, independent author. Many such bodies are overseeing conservative publishing policies and practices that fail to recognize how wathes of books are actually produced and sold, bought, and read in today's digital reading environment.

Reframing publishing and literary research and policy so that it properly accounts for how self-publishing authors *actually* work, trade, and negotiate today is a task that's now overdue.

ALLi's Self-Publishing 3.0 campaign recognizes the challenges today's authors face and works with writers and others to overcome them. Firstly, the campaign encourages authors to make the transition from being a content provider to running a business. To put the passion and mission that fires their books at the hub of their own literary enterprise.

The campaign also works with other author associations and representatives and literary, publishing, and creative industry organizations to foster author empowerment and entrepreneurial authorship—and to lobby the literary, publishing, and creative industries to support this shift.

Self-Publishing 3.0 recognizes that writing and publishing books is a long-term endeavor, that each author starts at zero and must produce the first words, then the first book, and then continuously develop their books and their business. It acknowledges that publishing is always a team effort, as much for the author–publisher as for any publishing house, and that good self-publishing services and assistance are key to sustainable success in publishing today.

More than anyone else in the publishing sector, the indie author is key to unfolding a new, more diverse, more accessible, and more equitable publishing landscape.

Author Empowerment

As we concluded in Chapter 2, the solution to author poverty is author empowerment. What does that mean, in practical terms?

• Author empowerment from the perspective of **a self-publishing writer** is the process of becoming stronger and more confident in claiming intellectual property and publishing rights and setting up effective writing and publishing processes.

• Author empowerment from the perspective of **author associations and representatives** is a set of measures designed to increase authors' autonomy and self-determination, so they can act from their own authority and represent their own interests in a responsible, self-determined way.

• Author empowerment from the perspective of **publishers and**

other rights buyers is meeting writers as business partners rather than content providers.

As the publishing landscape continues to reconfigure, the authors who are benefitting most are those who have developed an independent, creative, and empowered mindset. Only such a mindset can benefit from the unprecedented opportunities provided by today's publishing ecosystem.

Those authors who know how to exploit the commercial and creative value embedded in their intellectual property, those who have figured out who their readers are, what they want, and how to serve them, will thrive in the Self-Publishing 3.0 era. This is now well underway. The author community is growing in number, skill, and confidence. And a band of self-confident, skilled authors is an unstoppable force.

As the cap-in-hand, publish-me-please mindset fades in the author community, as increasing numbers of authors take up the challenge of developing publishing and business skills, as literary organizations and author representative bodies provide what's needed, we expand our collective sense of what's possible.

Self-Publishing 4.0

Self-publishing 3.0 was born out of what we colloquially call "The Cloud" —through SaaS (software as a service) tools: publishing platforms like Amazon KDP and Google Play, consumption tools like Amazon Prime and Audible, collaboration tools like Google Drive and Asana. Such tools are digital, but they also intersect with the physical world. You can upload a file to Amazon KDPP today and order a paperback book that will be delivered through to your letterbox via Amazon Prime tomorrow.

The next wave of technological change sweeping the publishing industry is artificial intelligence (AI), specifically **AI-As-A-Service**. As the internet revolutionized publishing in the first two decades of the twenty-first century, so AI-based solutions are already starting to transform publishing in the 2020s.

Services like Amazon's AWS, Google Cloud AI, or Microsoft Azure already offer natural language processing, document analysis, text extraction, translation, text-to-speech and speech-to-text, and other tools powered or augmented by AI. GPT (Generative Pre-trained Transformer), currently in its third iteration as **GPT-3**, is a language prediction model created by the San Francisco research lab OpenAI, and currently producing text—fiction, nonfiction, and poetry—that is ever more human-like and useful.

Another technology that is potentially transformative is **blockchain**, a specific type of database stored as a growing list of records, called blocks that are linked using cryptography. Blockchain makes the history of any digital asset unalterable and transparent and, again depending on authors' sense of their own value and self-worth, it has the potential to intensify and accelerate pro-author trends in the coming years, enabling writers to invent new offerings, reach more readers worldwide, and get paid in more advantageous ways.

If you are interested you can explore more about the potential of blockchain in self-publishing in **Blockchain for Books campaign** and our short guide *Authors and The Blockchain*.

How quickly can we move our thought patterns and mindsets to meet the potential of the abundance of new technology now available to us? Today in the era of Self-Publishing 3.0, many authors are still in self-publishing 1.0 activities: paying a publishing partner to produce a print book and paying for PR traditional media campaigns. Many others are just dipping their toes into Self-Publishing 2.0, and coming to understand what's possible for them through digital publishing, but not yet thinking of themselves as creative business owners.

Those self-publishing authors who have worked out what publishing tech and services can do for them and have adopted savvy publishing practices can look forward to further improvements in income and influence as Self-Publishing enters the 4.0 era.

Right now, it's up to authors to build the framework of creative and commercial independence that will allow the most purposeful, profitable, and pleasurable connections with their readers. That is the great freedom, and the great responsibility, we have been granted today.

THE END

REVIEW REQUEST
WE'D LOVE YOUR FEEDBACK

If you enjoyed or benefitted from this book, please could you leave a brief review online? A good review is very important to authors these days as it helps other readers know whether a book worth their time.

It doesn't have to be long or detailed. Just a sentence saying what you enjoyed and a star-rating is all that's needed. Many thanks.

- *Review on Amazon.com*
- *Review on Apple Books*
- *Review on Goodreads*
- *Review on Google Books*
- *Review on Kobo*
- *Review on ALLi's Self-Publishing Advice Centre Bookstore*

SELF-PUBLISHING NEWS & ADVICE

We'd love to send you a weekly roundup of news and advice for indie authors. Delivered to your inbox each Wednesday.

Sign up for top tips and tools from the Alliance of Independent Authors

AllianceIndependentAuthors.org/roundup

ACKNOWLEDGMENTS

All good books are a team effort. Behind the author's name on the cover and the words within is the creative team of editors and designers and formatters who made the book, the distributors and marketers who take it to readers, and the long list of supporters—from family to colleagues—without whom it could never have been created. Then there are all the other authors, journalists, researchers, storytellers, and poets who have contributed the ideas, information, and inspirations that an author draws on, consciously or unconsciously. I am grateful to all.

For this short guide, particular thanks are due to editors Eliza Dee at Clio Editing and Lauren Johnson Wordsmith, to designer Jane Dixon-Smith, and to ALLi enterprise advisor Joanna Penn, with whom I worked out many of the ideas contained here. For this book and all our work together: thank you.

Personal thanks are due to Sarah Begley for her publishing assistance. Thank you Sarah for your unfailing patience and formidable organization skills.

And to the members, subscribers, followers, ambassadors, and advisors at ALLi, the Alliance of Independent Authors. Like our other ALLi guides and resources, this book relies on your experiences, the knowledge and wisdom you so generously share in our community through case histories on our blog, discussions in our ALLi member forums, and inspirational interviews on our podcast. Thank you for making this book, and our organization, possible. And for the generosity, enthusiasm, and kindness that makes going to work each day pure pleasure.

ABOUT ALLI

ALLi, the Alliance of Independent Authors, is the global, professional association for self-publishing indie authors.

Join us for reliable advice and advocacy, discounts, guidebooks and resources, member forums, contract reviews, and support from a dedicated indie author community.

AllianceIndependentAuthors.org

facebook.com/AllianceIndieAuthors
twitter.com/indieauthoralli

Self-Publishing 3.0
Author Empowerment through Creative Business

© 2020 Orna A Ross
Alliance of Independent Authors

Ebook: 978-1-913349-41-7
Paperback: 978-1-913349-42-4
Large Print: 978-1-913349-44-8
HB: 978-1-913349-43-1
Audio: 978-1-913349-45-5

The moral rights of the author have been asserted. All rights reserved.

Enquiries: info@ornaross.com

❉ Created with Vellum

FontPublications

FONT PUBLICATIONS IS THE PUBLISHING IMPRINT
FOR ORNA ROSS FICTION AND POETRY
AND THE ALLIANCE OF INDEPENDENT AUTHORS
PUBLISHING GUIDES FOR AUTHORS & POETS

ALL FONT BOOKS—FICTION, NONFICTION, AND POETRY—HAVE THE SAME INTENTION AT SOURCE: TO INSPIRE CREATIVE INDEPENDENCE, EMOTIONAL FREEDOM, AND IMAGINATIVE CONNECTION.

NOTES

1. The Enterprising Author

1. Joshua Yuvaraj and Rebecca Giblin. 2019. "Are Contracts Enough?" Melbourne University Law Review, Vol. 44, No. 1, 2020
2. Diminishing Returns: Creative Culture at Risk (2018) Report on income survey of Canadian writers
3. Horizon Research Writers' Earnings in New Zealand (2017) https://www.internationalauthors.org/wp-content/uploads/2017/10/Horizon-NZ-Writers-Earnings-Survey-2016.pdf
4. UK Authors' Earnings and Contracts (2018) A Survey of 50,000 Writers
5. Arts Council EnglandLiterature in the 21st Century: Understanding Models of Support for Literary Fiction
6.
7. https://www.forbes.com/sites/niallmccarthy/2019/01/09/u-s-authors-have-suffered-a-drastic-decline-in-earnings-infographic/?sh=15b23f1d655e
8. The Authors Guild. (2018) Author Income Survey.
9. *janefriedman.com/author-income-surveys/*

2. The road to Self-Publishing 3.0

1. Bob Brown. 1930. *The Readies*.

10. Author Special Sales

1. http://community.bookapss.org/page/what-is-special-sales

11. Developing A Fan Base

1. https://a16z.com/2020/02/06/100-true-fans/